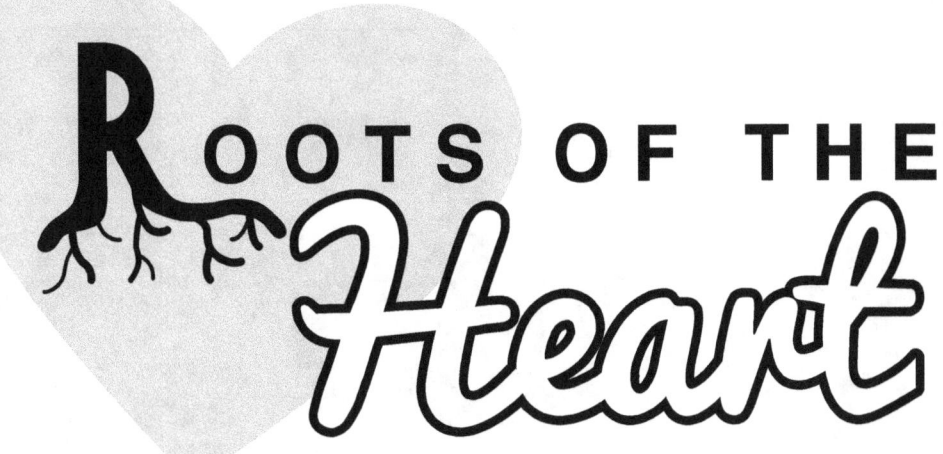

Roots of the Heart

A coloring adventure for all

Jeanette Wummel

Coloring Tip:

When coloring with markers place a piece of paper between pages to prevent bleeding to your next design.

Acknowledgments

I can never say thank you to all the people who have supported and encourage me in making my dreams come true.

I dedicate this book to my grandmother, who was more like a mom to me. She has the kindest heart and always see the best in everyone. She taught me that if I was ever lonely all I had to do was put my finger out and I could feel her love shield around me.

I also would like to dedicate this book to my husband who has captured my heart.

Copyright

Published by The Roots of Design www.TheRootsOfDesign.com

Designs: Jeanette Wummel

ISBN-10:0-9968479-6-0
ISBN-13:978-0-9968479-6-4

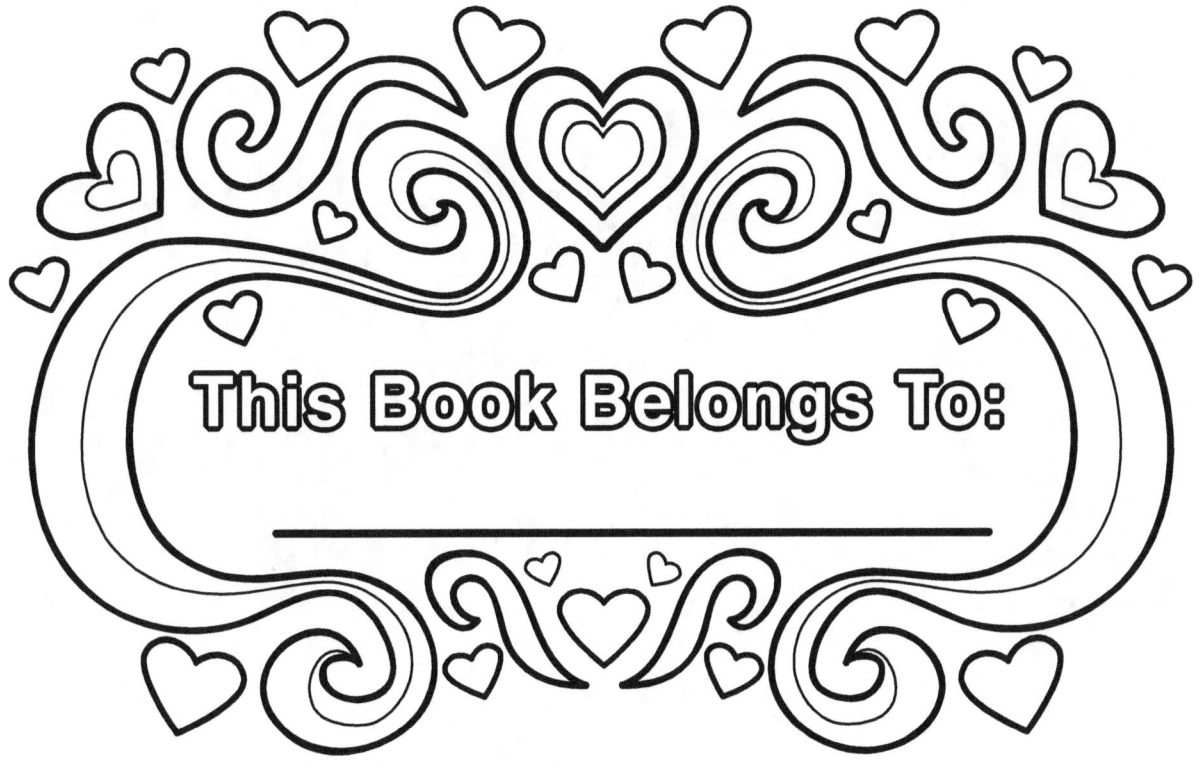

This Book Belongs To:

_____

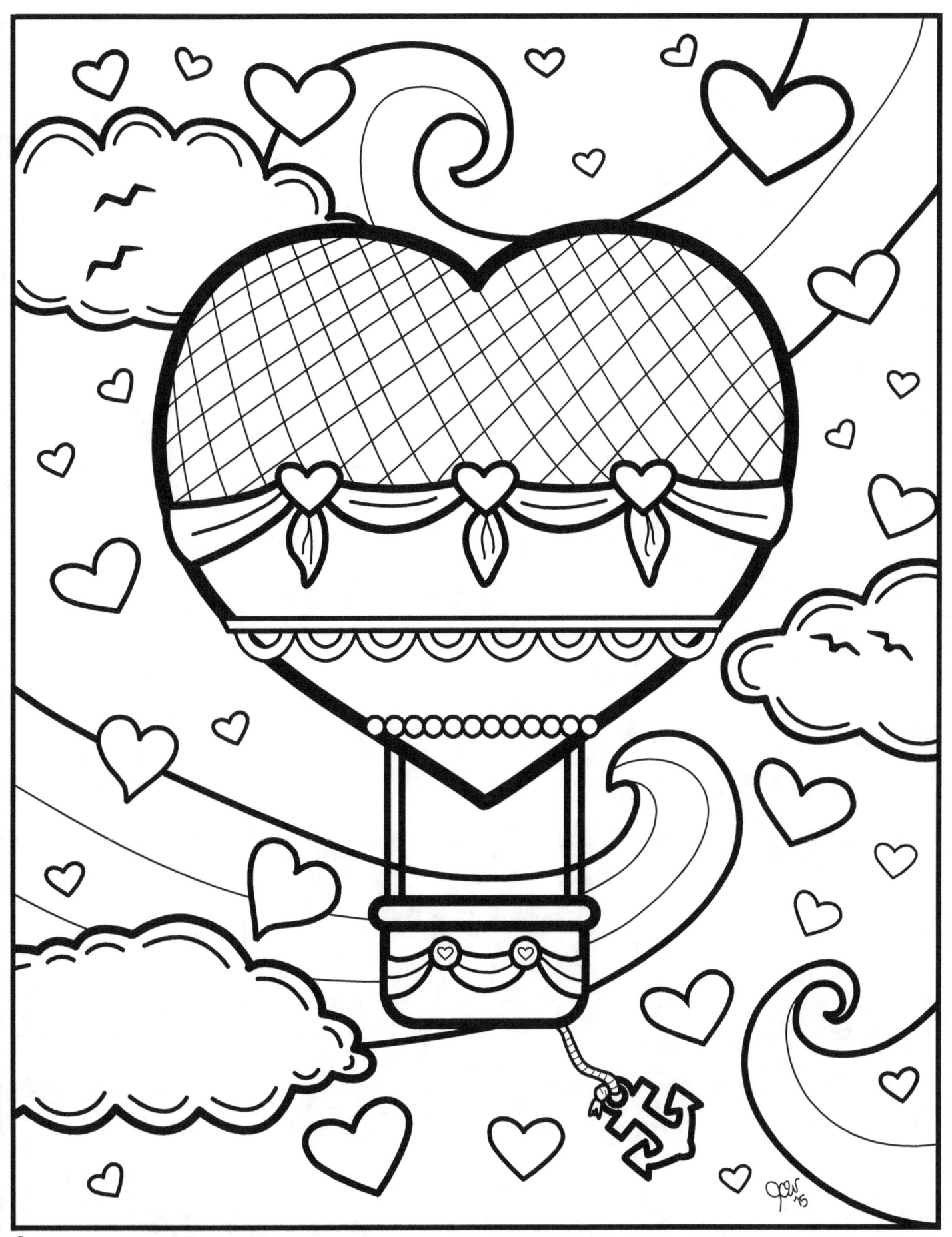

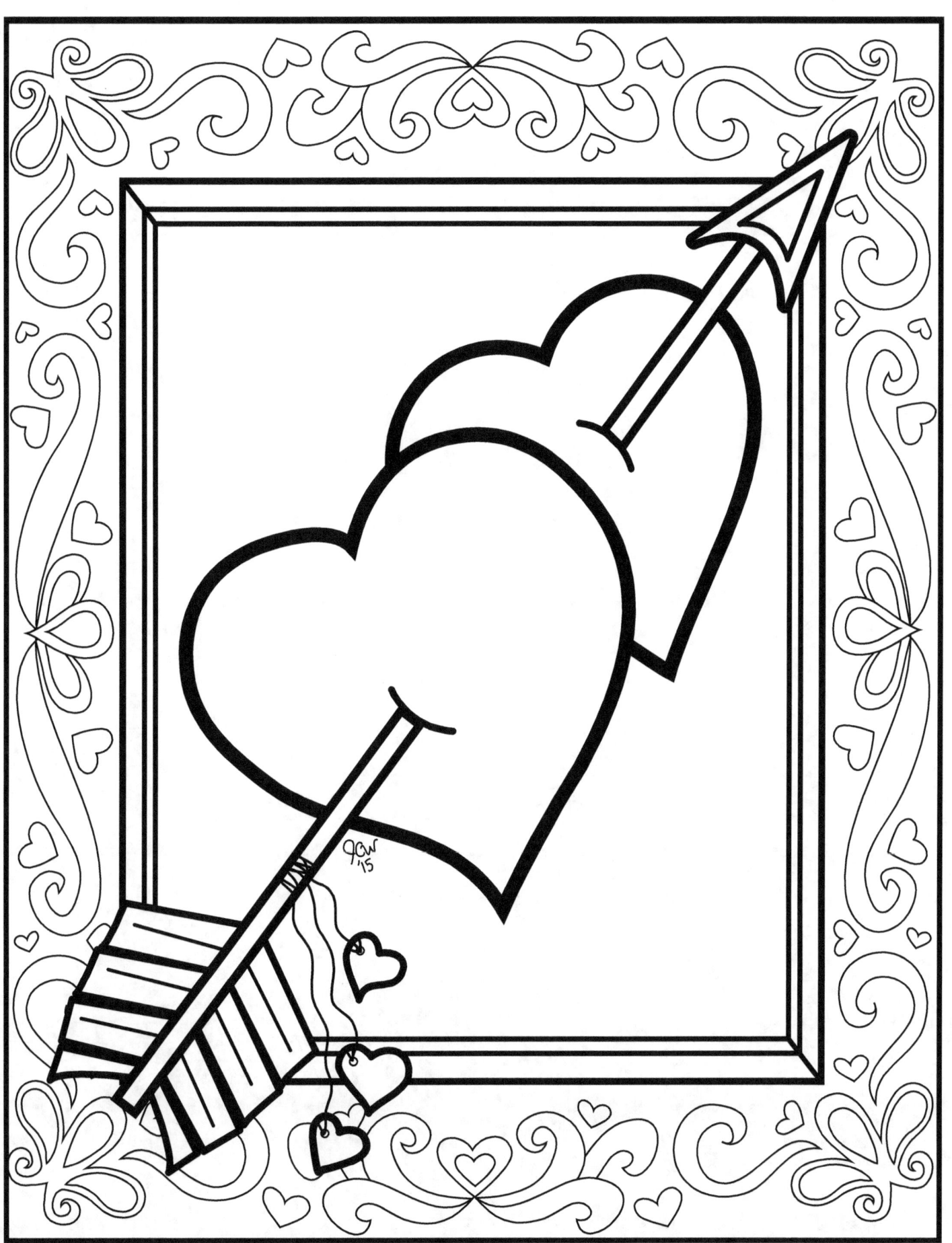

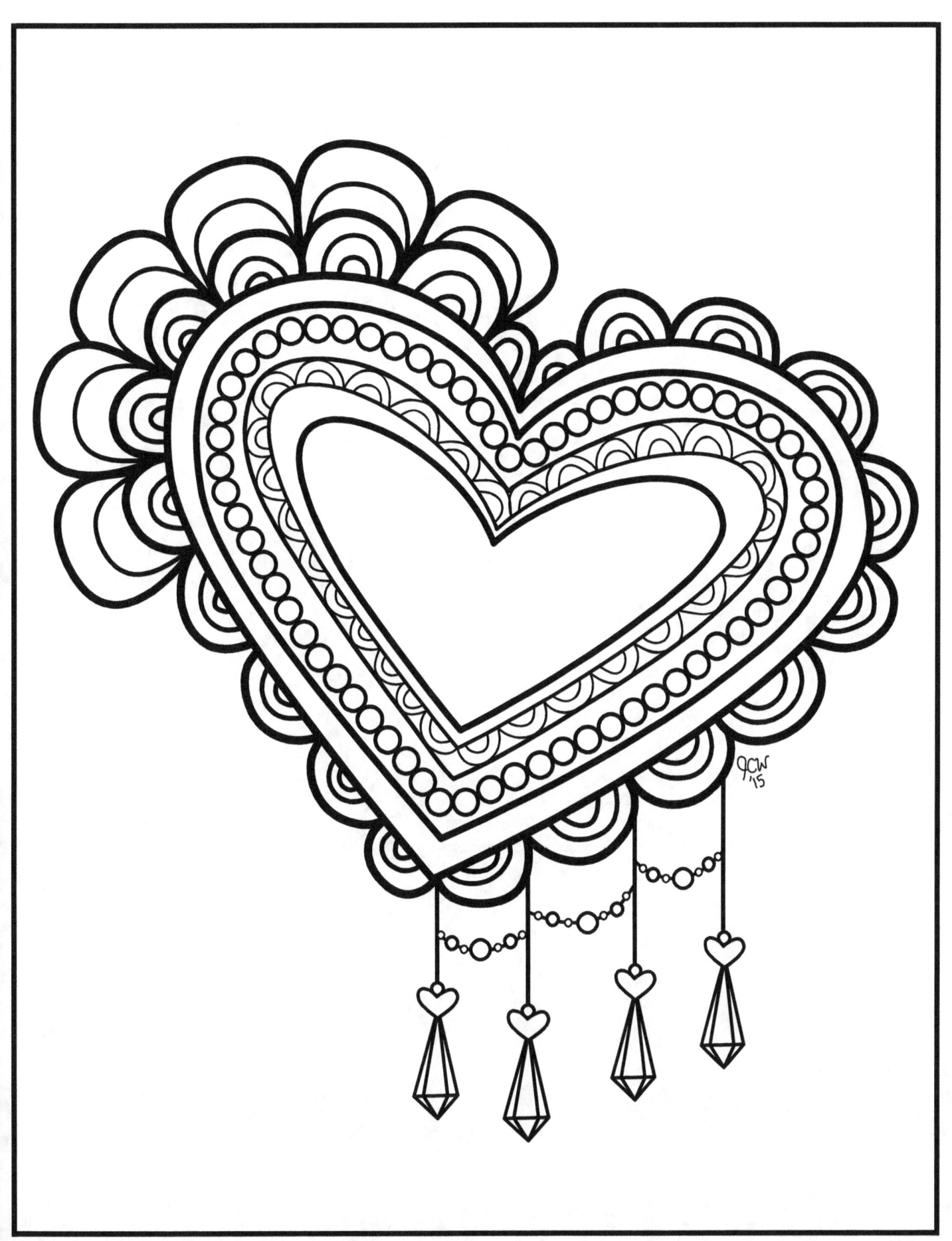

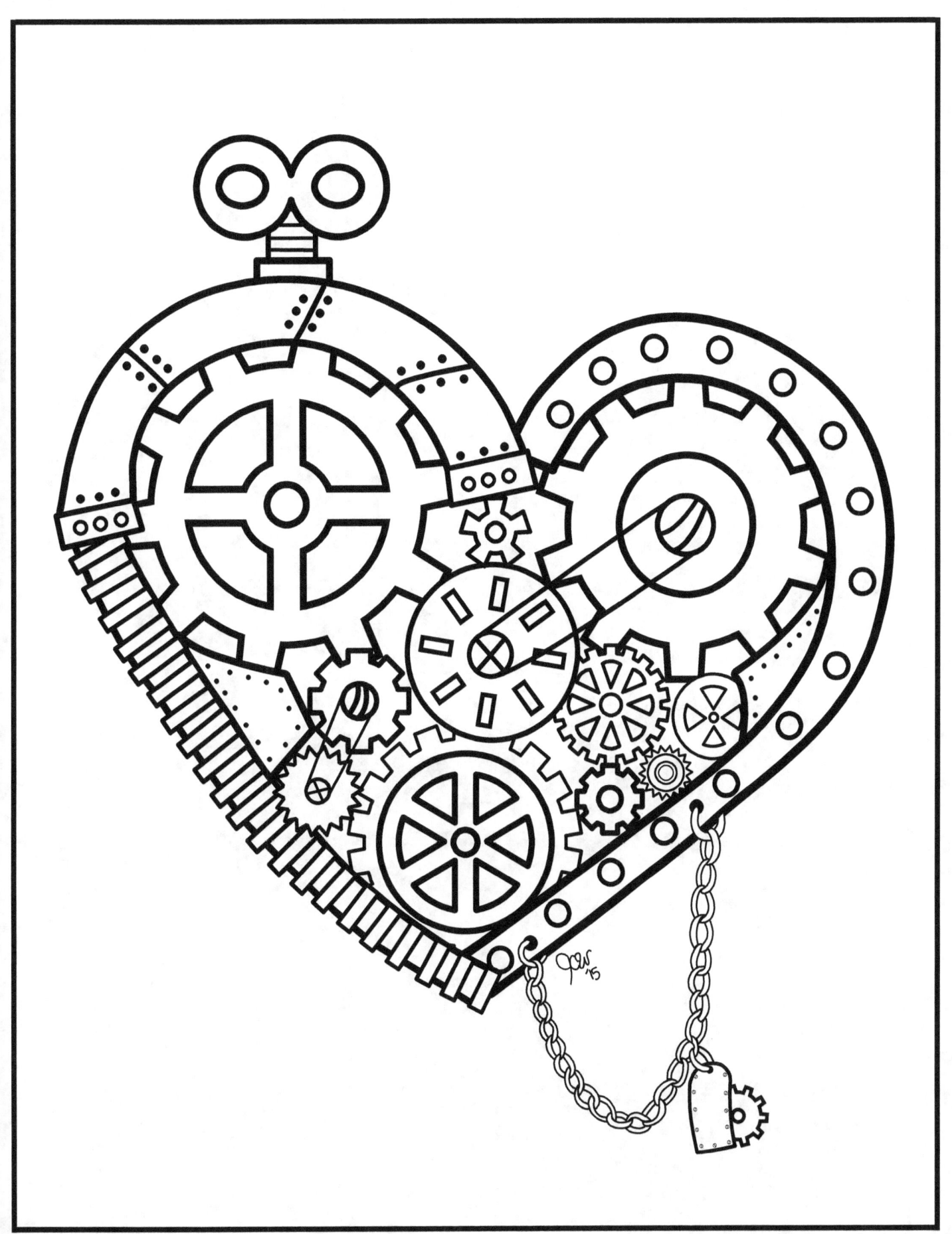

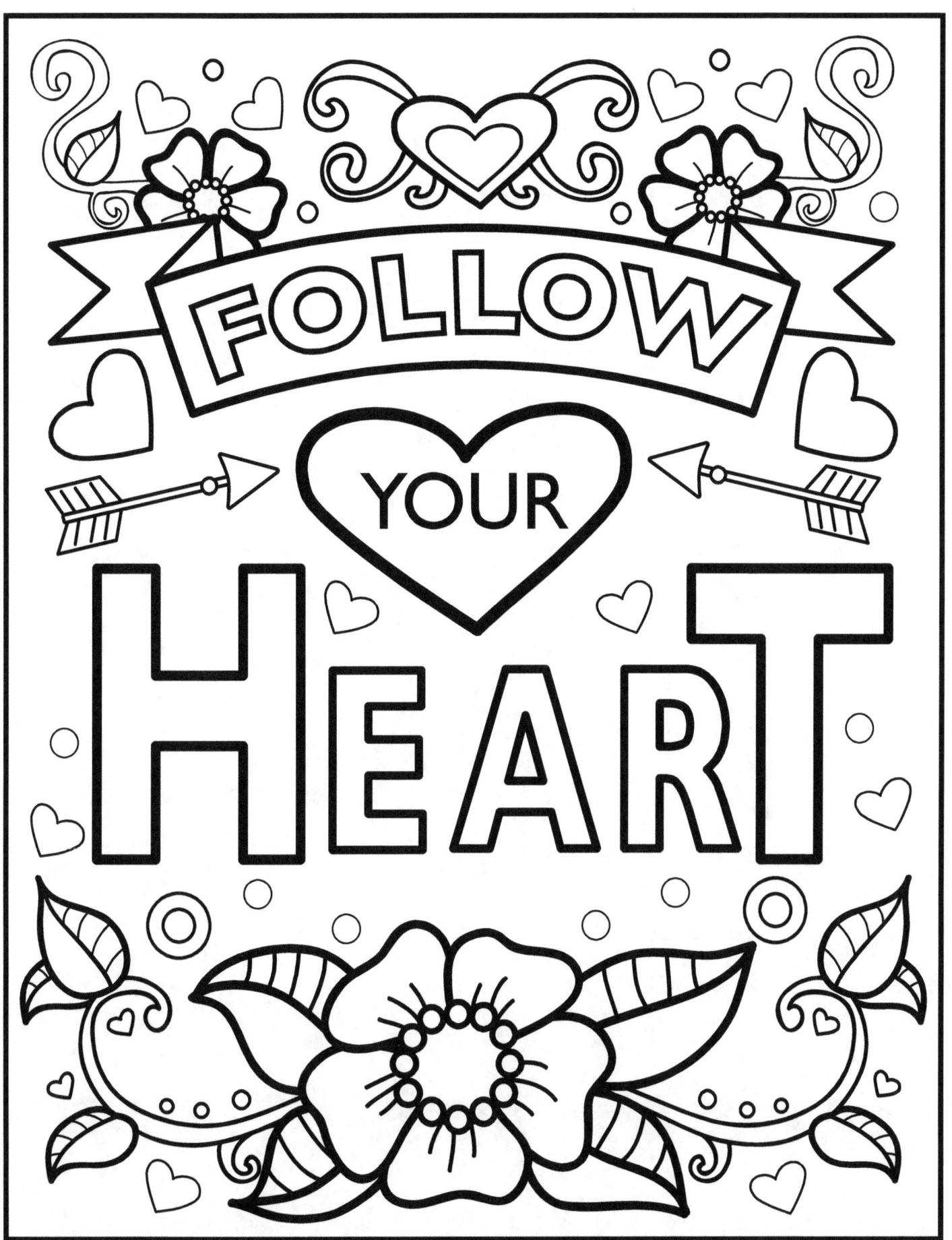

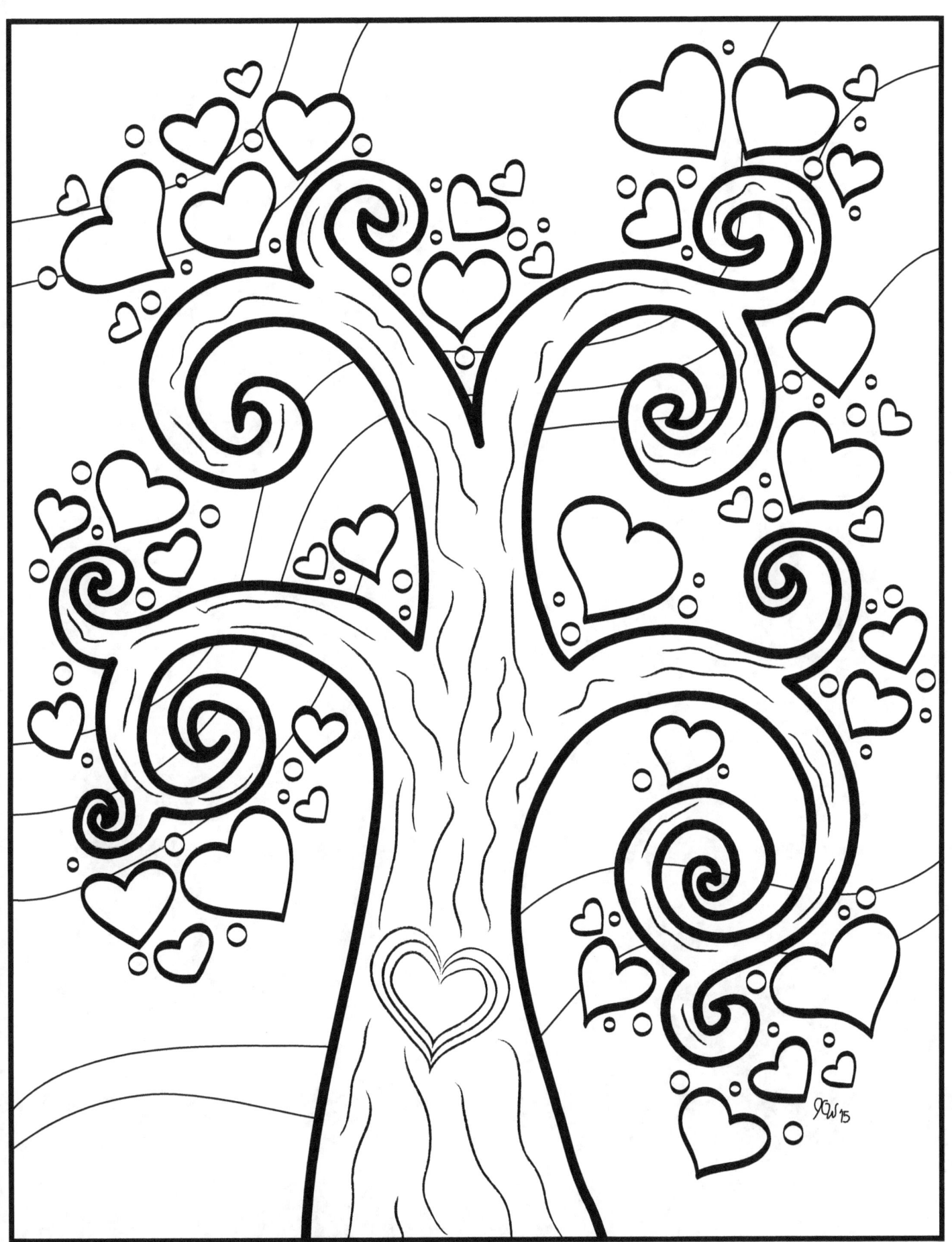

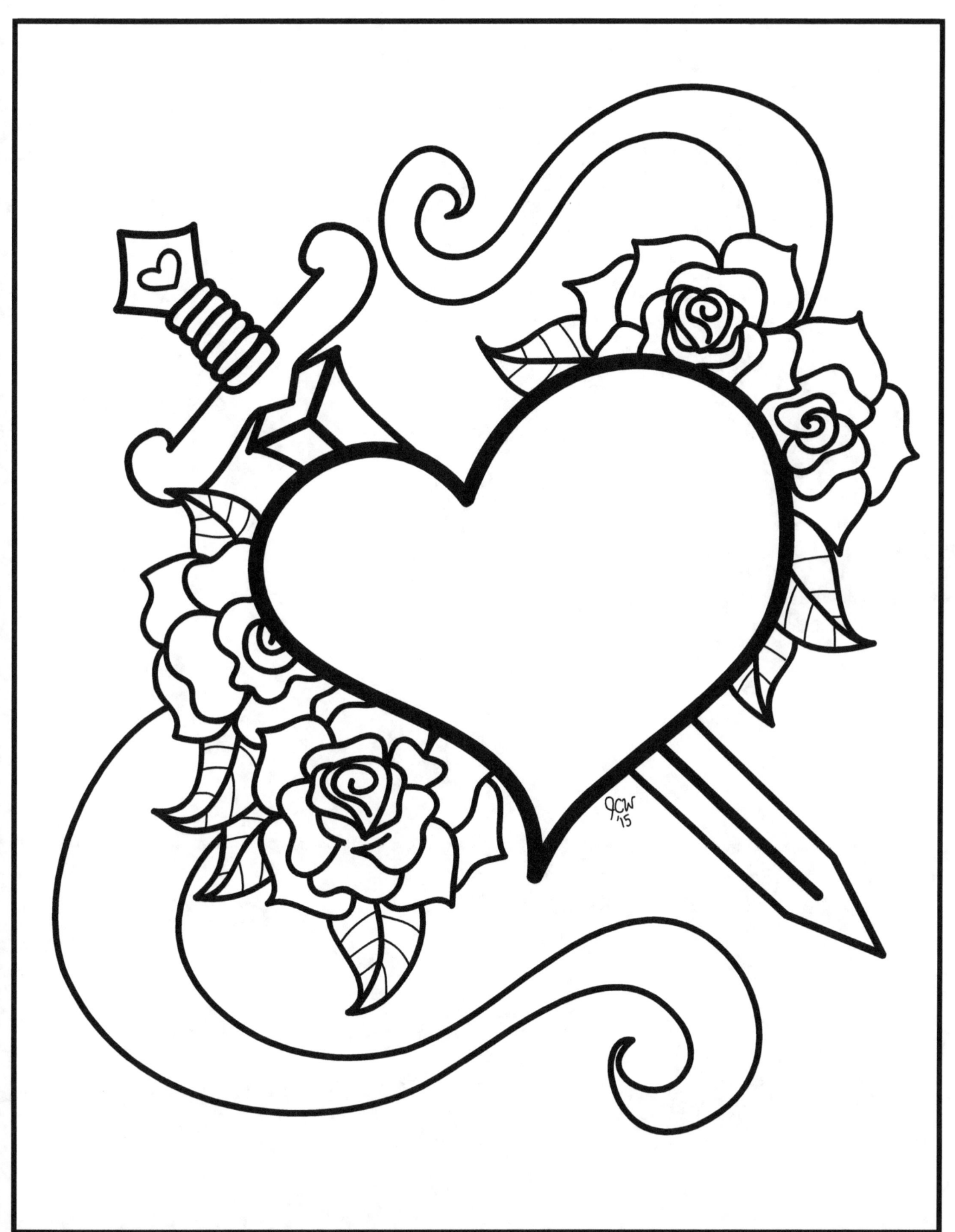

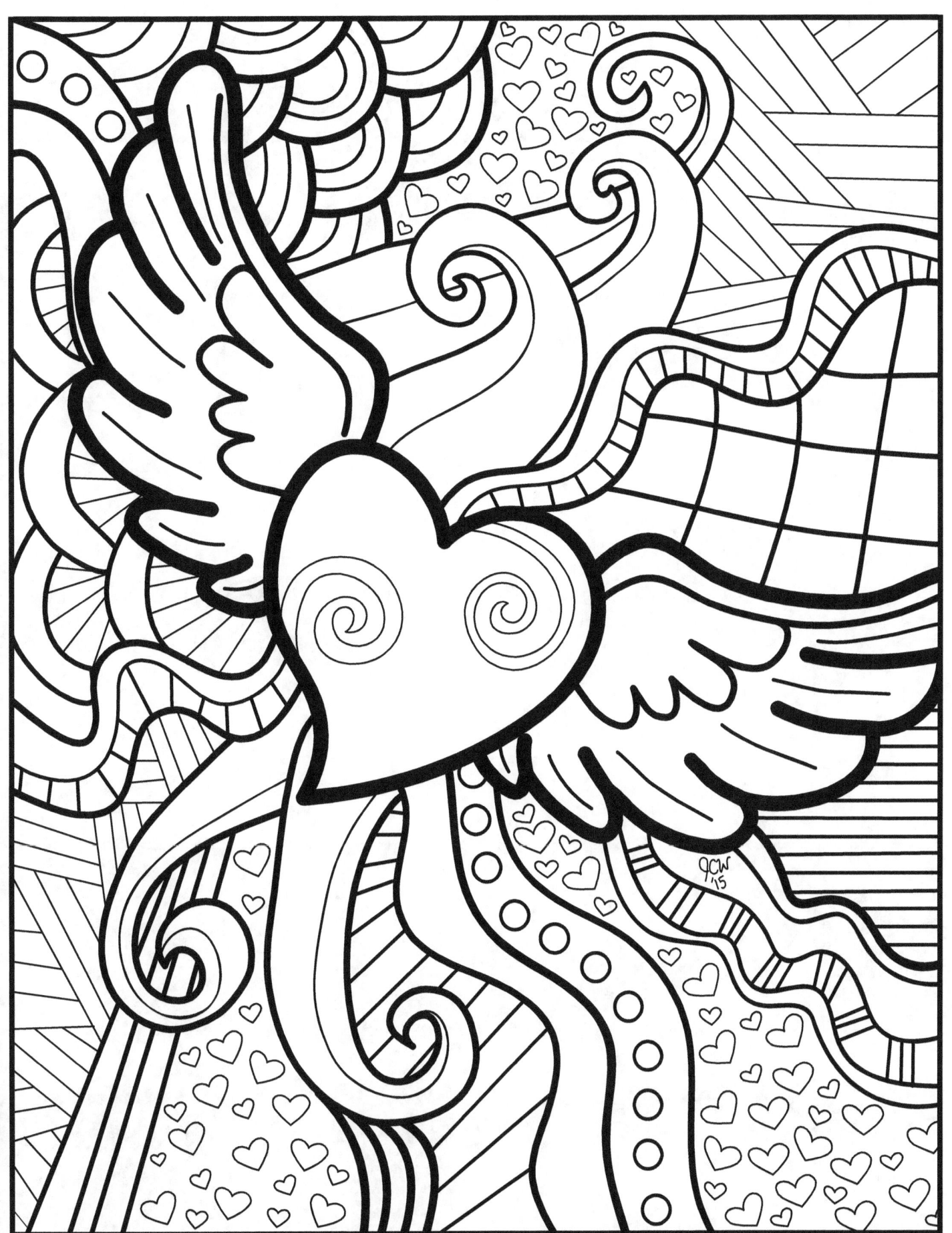

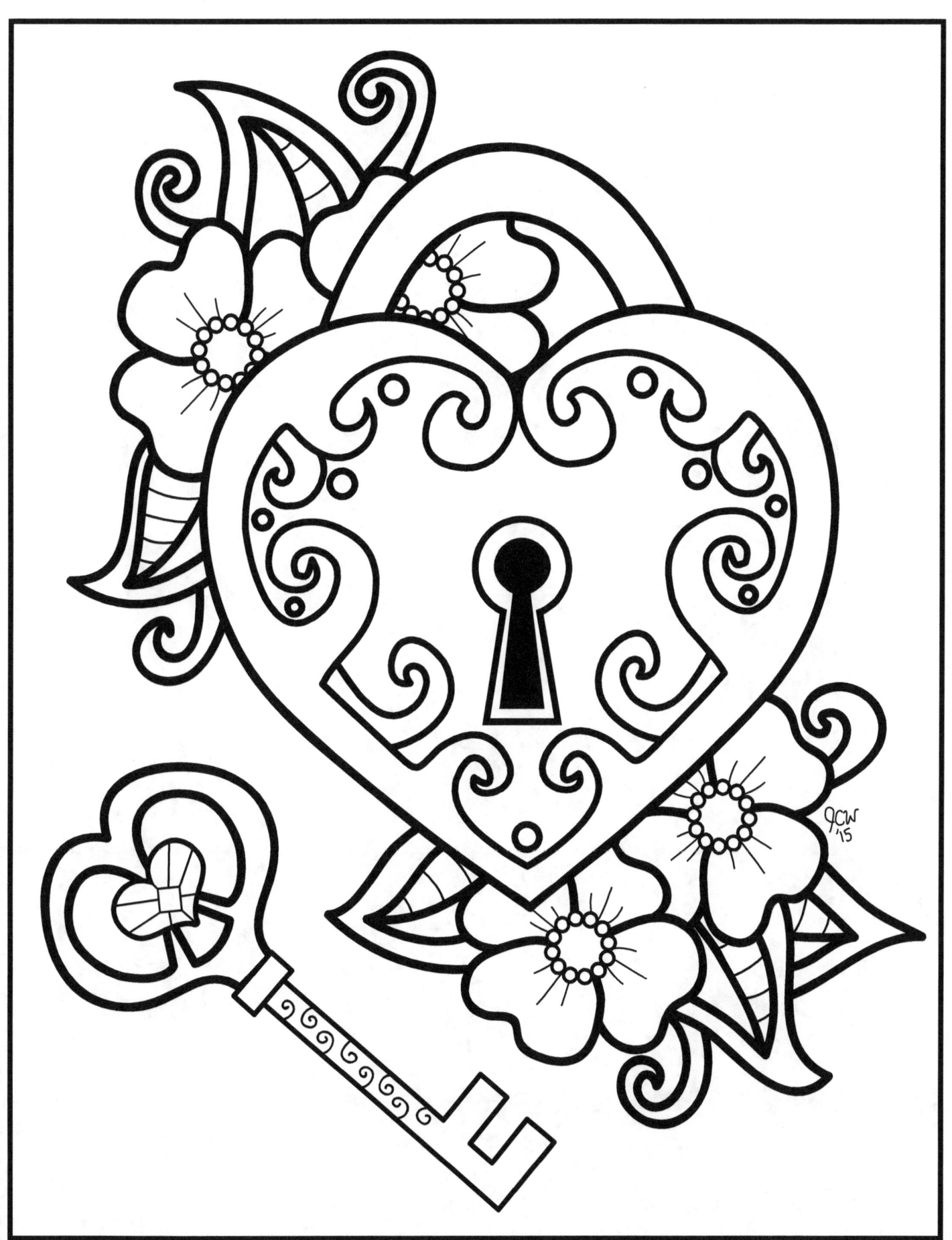

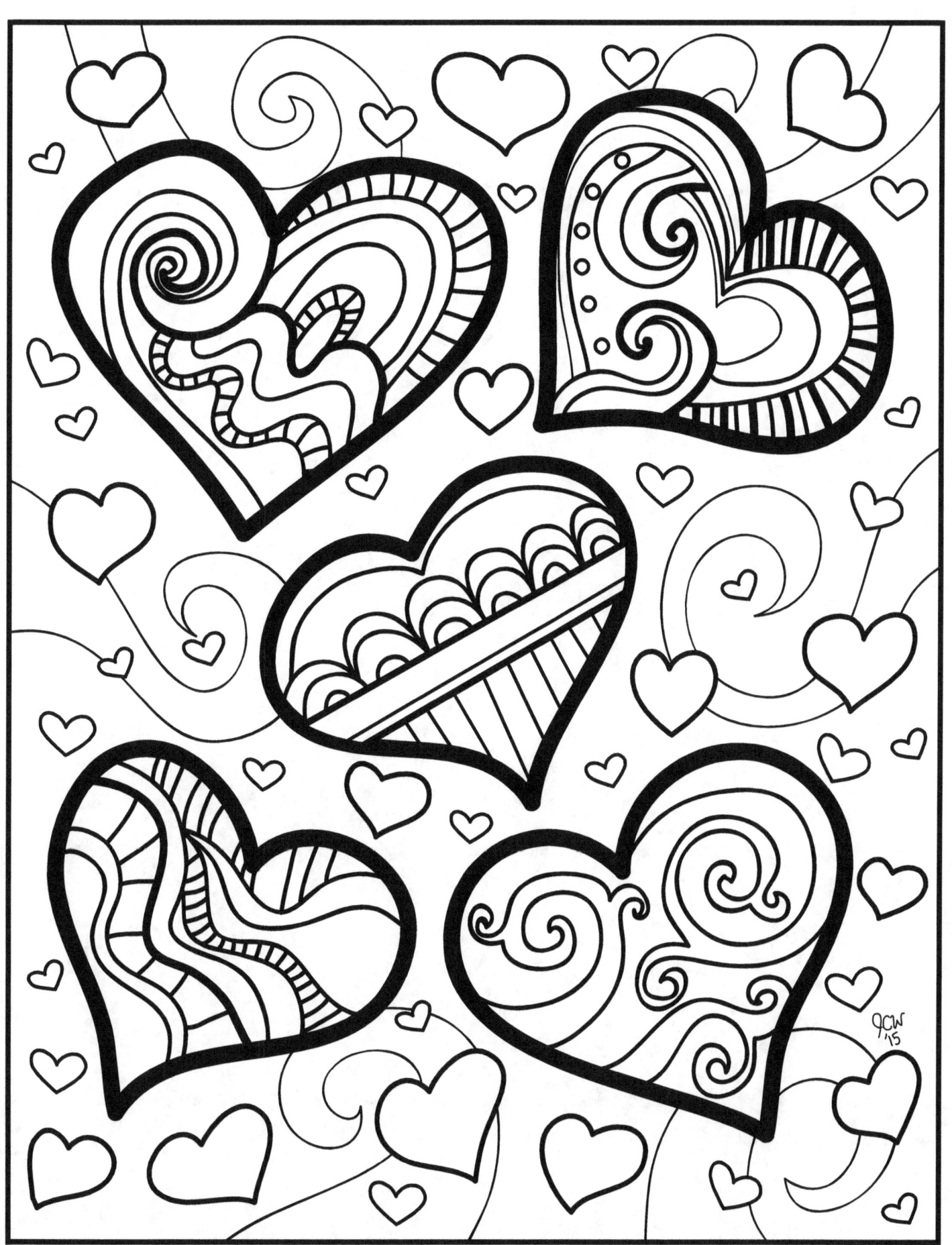

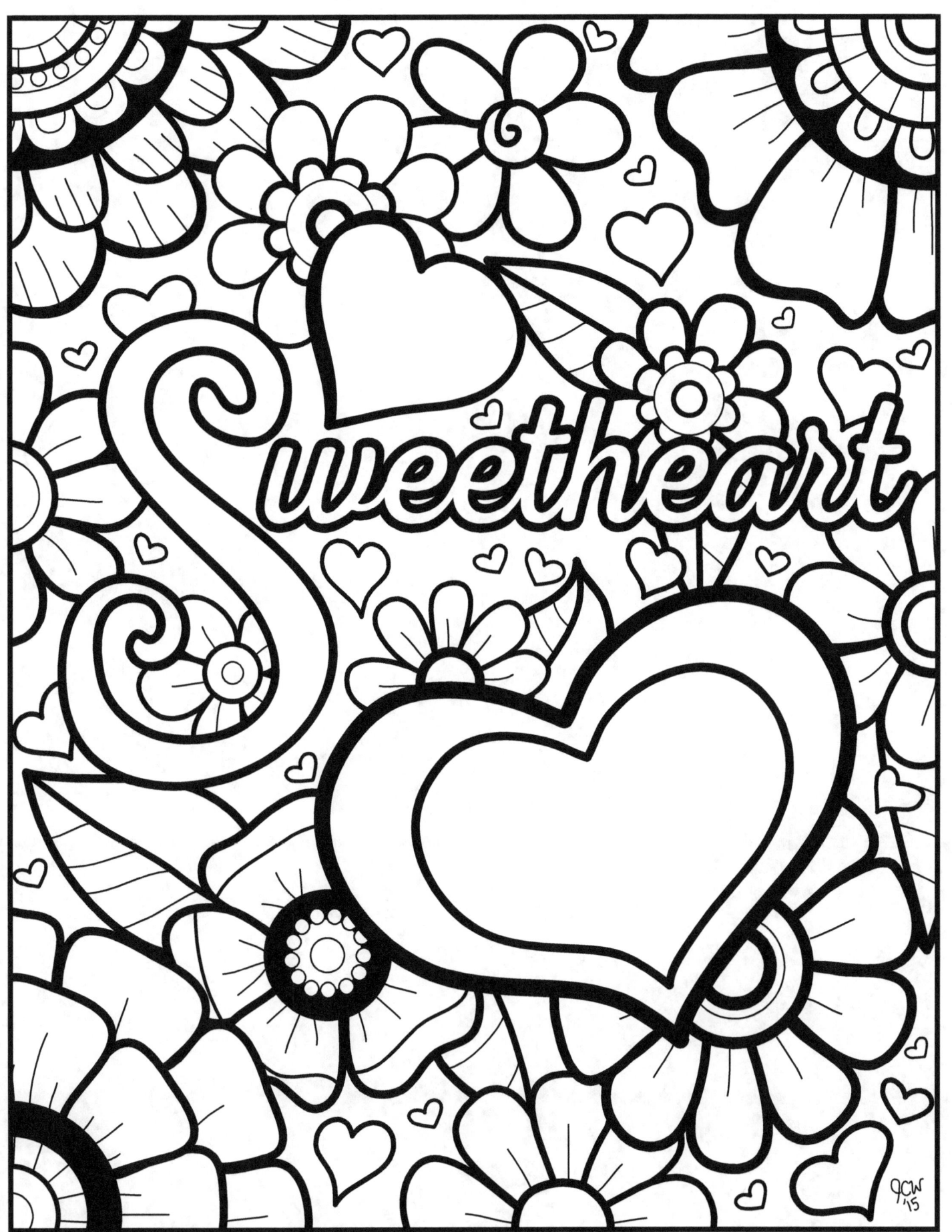

Sweetheart

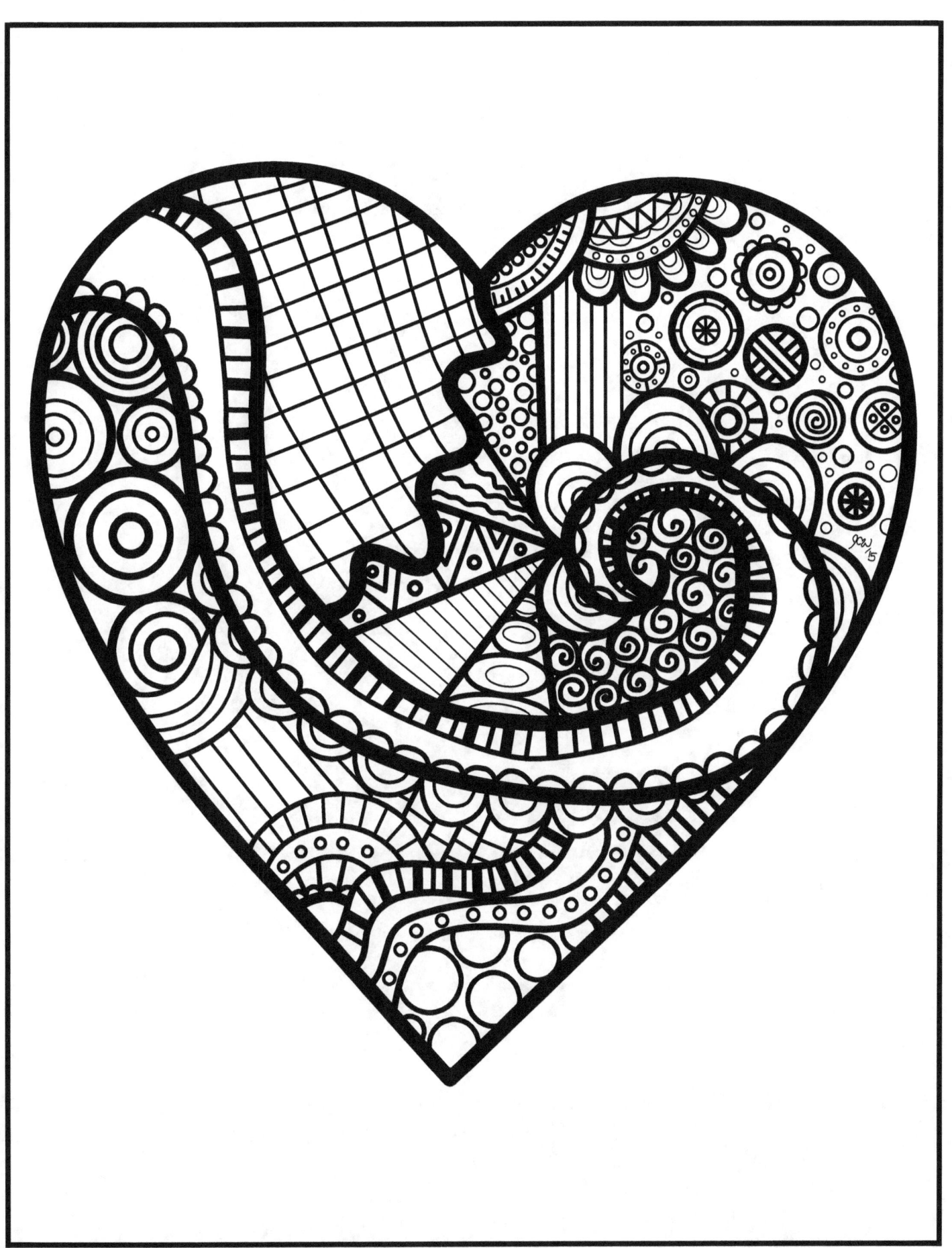

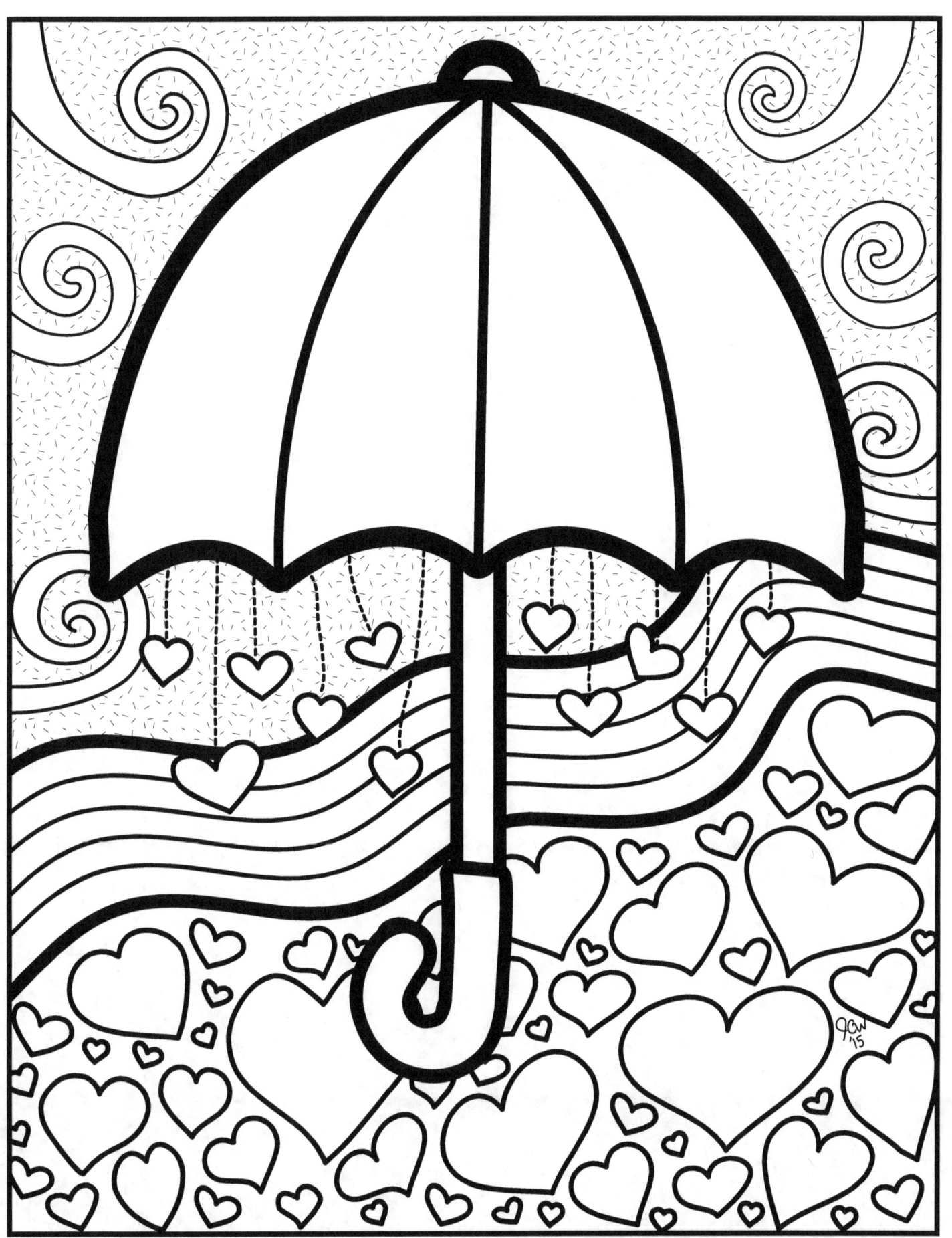

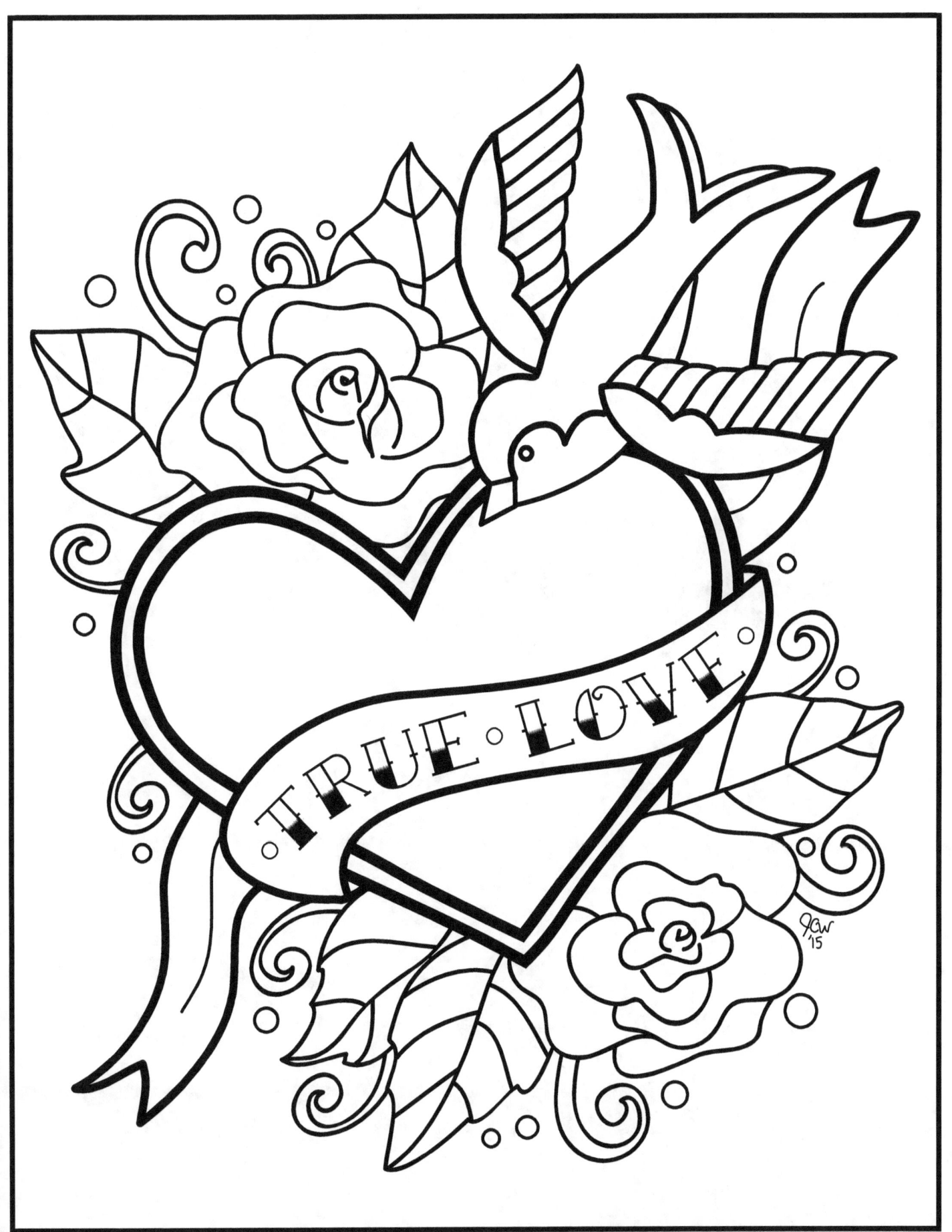

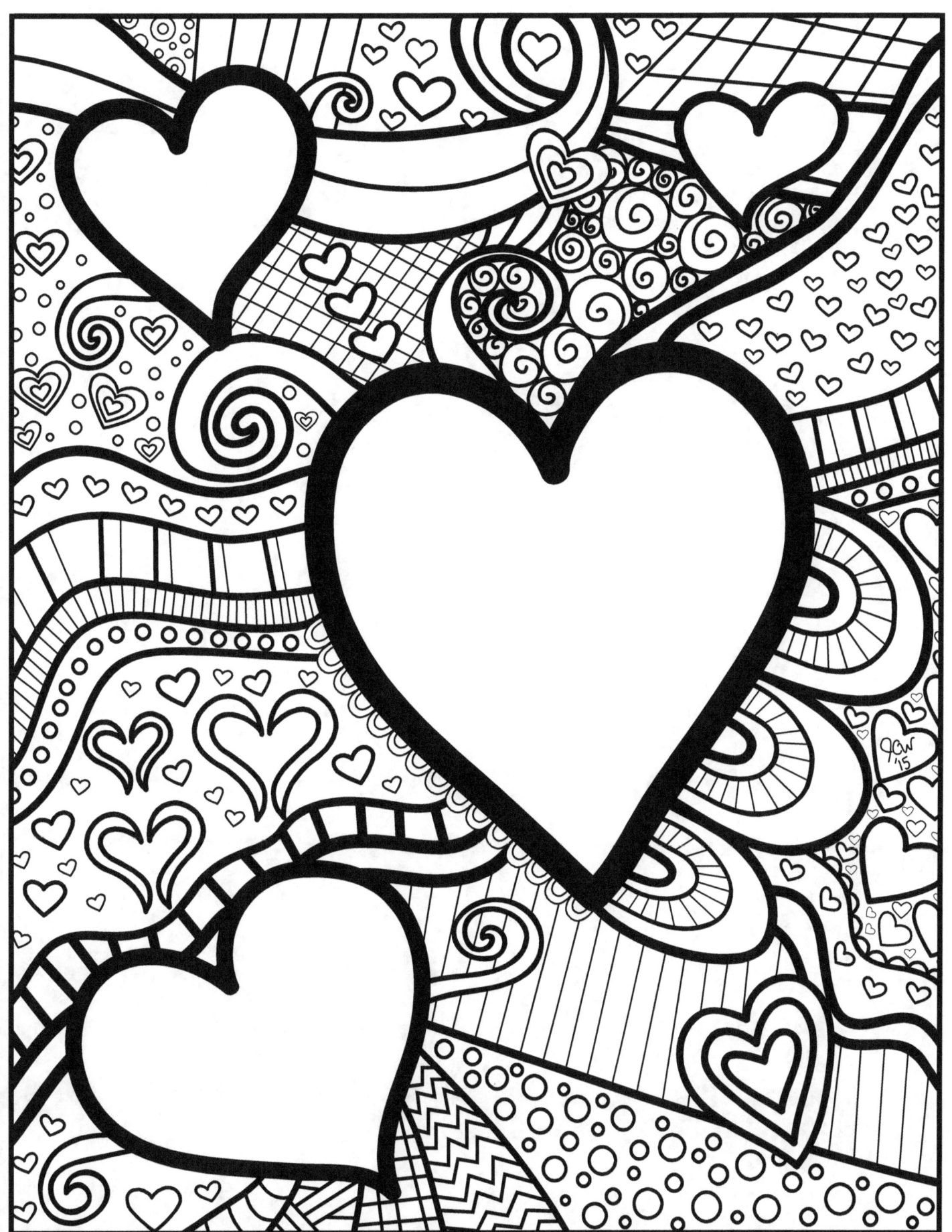

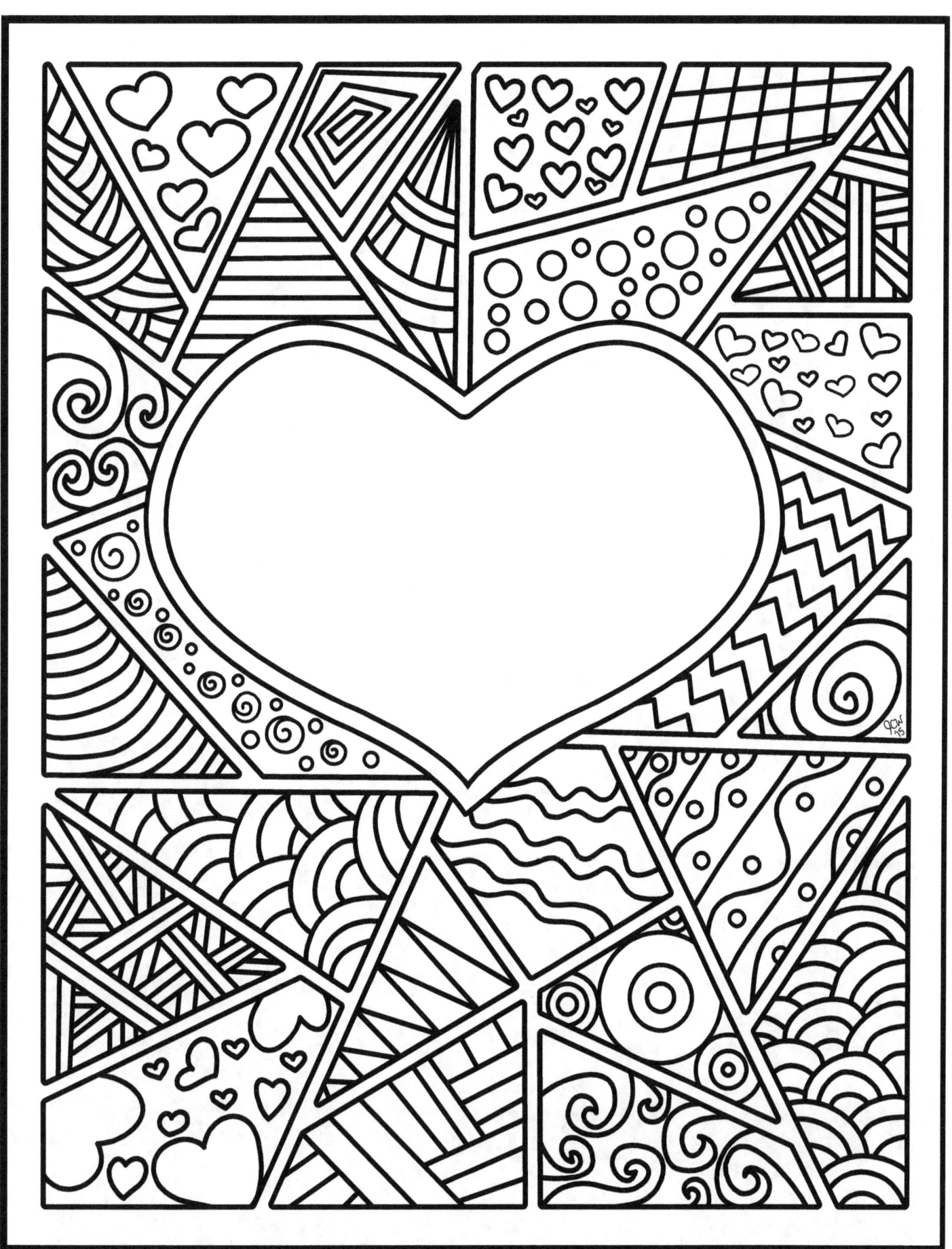

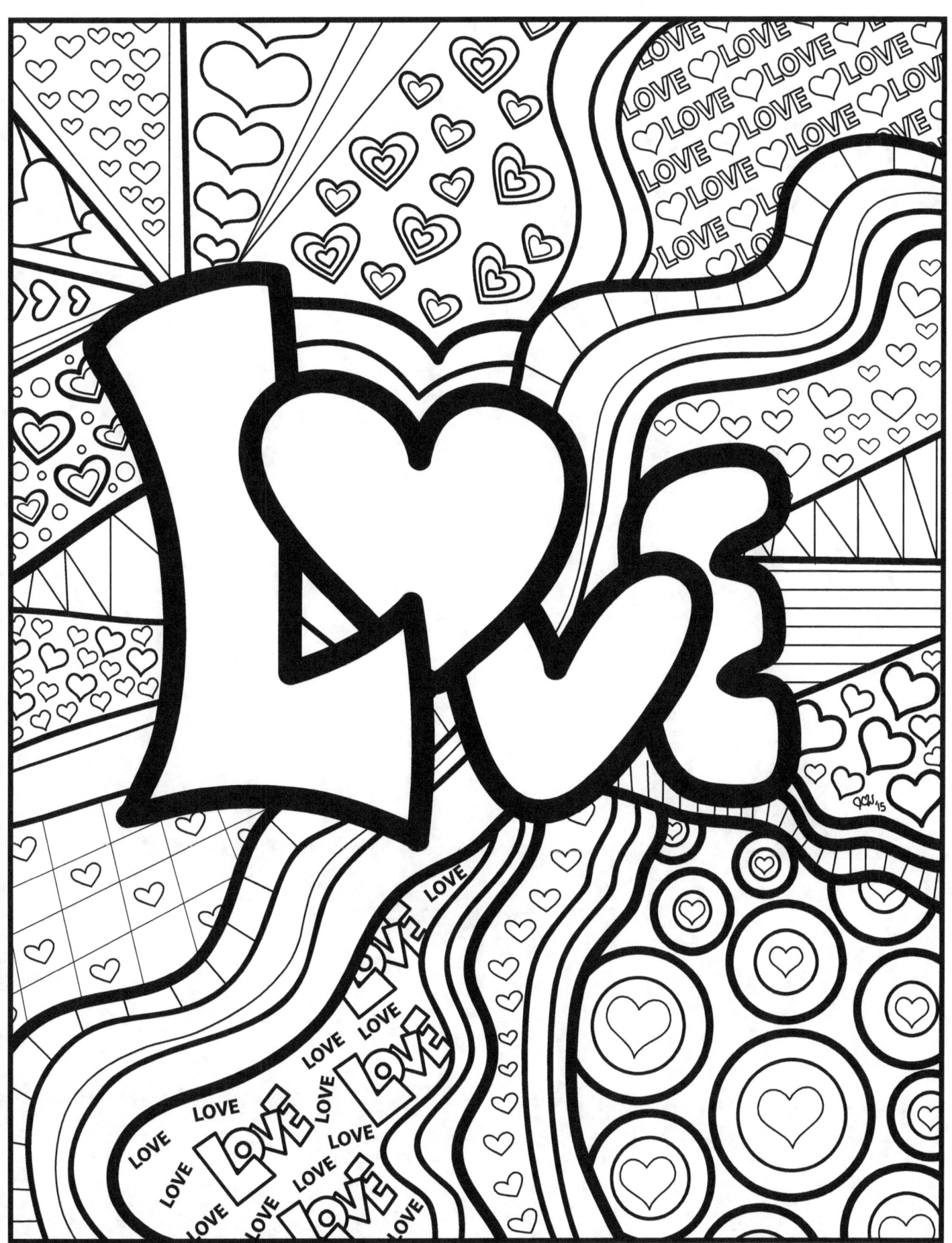

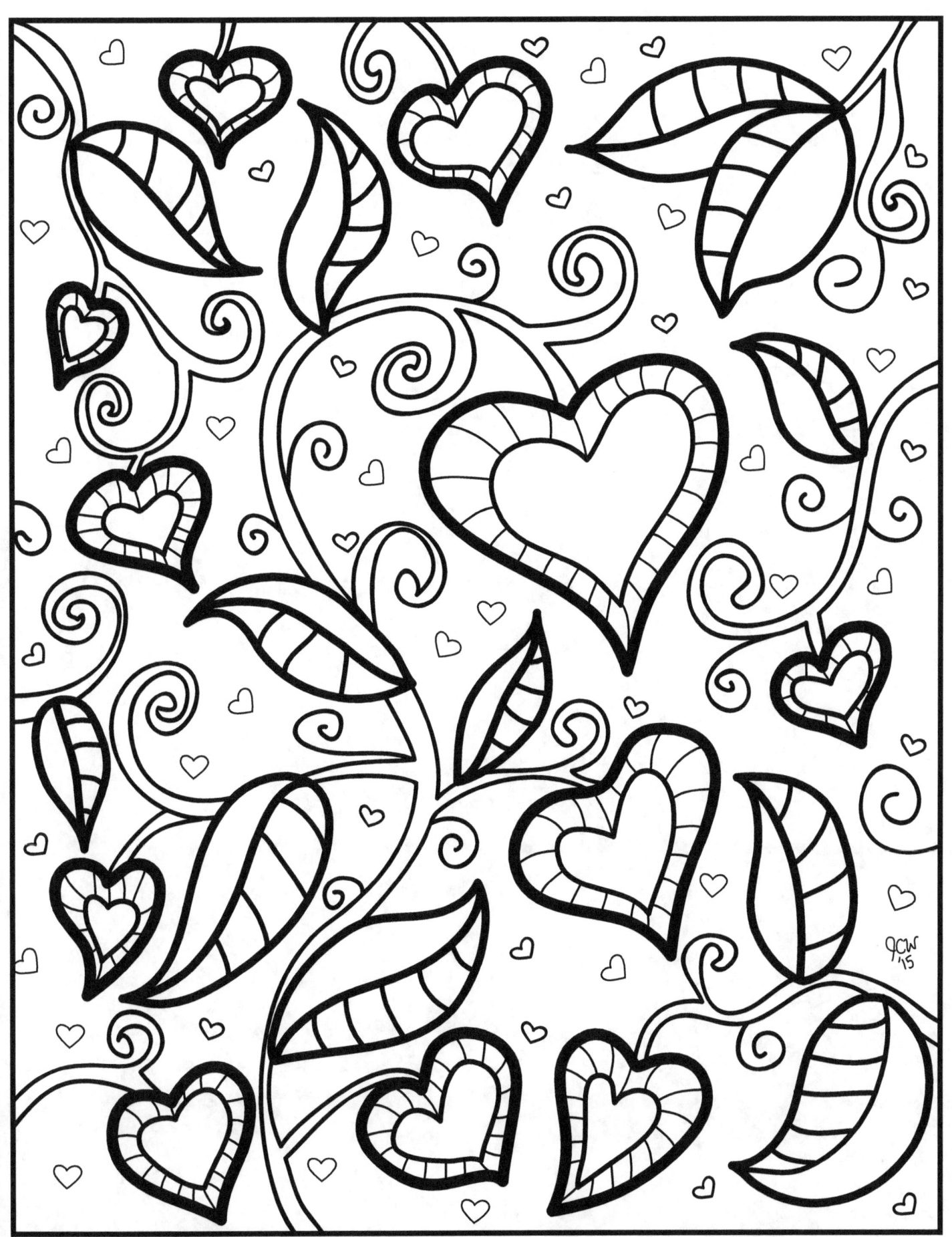